THE ADVENTURES OF ROCKY & SKYE

A one-act comedy by
Kelly DuMar

www.youthplays.com
info@youthplays.com
424-703-5315

The Adventures of Rocky & Skye © 2009 Kelly DuMar
All rights reserved. ISBN 978-1-62088-026-5.

Caution: This play is fully protected under the copyright laws of the United States of America, Canada, the British Commonwealth and all other countries of the copyright union and is subject to royalty for all performances including but not limited to professional, amateur, charity and classroom whether admission is charged or presented free of charge.

Reservation of Rights: This play is the property of the author and all rights for its use are strictly reserved and must be licensed by his representative, YouthPLAYS. This prohibition of unauthorized professional and amateur stage presentations extends also to motion pictures, recitation, lecturing, public reading, radio broadcasting, television, video and the rights of adaptation or translation into non-English languages.

Performance Licensing and Royalty Payments: Amateur and stock performance rights are administered exclusively by YouthPLAYS. No amateur, stock or educational theatre groups or individuals may perform this play without securing authorization and royalty arrangements in advance from YouthPLAYS. Required royalty fees for performing this play are available online at www.YouthPLAYS.com. Royalty fees are subject to change without notice. Required royalties must be paid each time this play is performed and may not be transferred to any other performance entity. All licensing requests and inquiries should be addressed to YouthPLAYS.

Author Credit: All groups or individuals receiving permission to produce this play must give the author(s) credit in any and all advertisements and publicity relating to the production of this play. The author's billing must appear directly below the title on a separate line with no other accompanying written matter. The name of the author(s) must be at least 50% as large as the title of the play. No person or entity may receive larger or more prominent credit than that which is given to the author(s) and the name of the author(s) may not be abbreviated or otherwise altered from the form in which it appears in this Play.

Publisher Attribution: All programs, advertisements, flyers or other printed material must include the following notice:
    Produced by special arrangement with YouthPLAYS (www.youthplays.com).

Prohibition of Unauthorized Copying: Any unauthorized copying of this book or excerpts from this book, whether by photocopying, scanning, video recording or any other means, is strictly prohibited by law. This book may only be copied by licensed productions with the purchase of a photocopy license, or with explicit permission from YouthPLAYS.

Trade Marks, Public Figures & Musical Works: This play may contain references to brand names or public figures. All references are intended only as parody or other legal means of expression. This play may also contain suggestions for the performance of a musical work (either in part or in whole). YouthPLAYS has not obtained performing rights of these works unless explicitly noted. The direction of such works is only a playwright's suggestion, and the play producer should obtain such permissions on their own. The website for the U.S. copyright office is *http://www.copyright.gov*.

COPYRIGHT RULES TO REMEMBER

1. To produce this play, you must receive prior written permission from YouthPLAYS and pay the required royalty.

2. You must pay a royalty each time the play is performed in the presence of audience members outside of the cast and crew. Royalties are due whether or not admission is charged, whether or not the play is presented for profit, for charity or for educational purposes, or whether or not anyone associated with the production is being paid.

3. No changes, including cuts or additions, are permitted to the script without written prior permission from YouthPLAYS.

4. Do not copy this book or any part of it without written permission from YouthPLAYS.

5. Credit to the author and YouthPLAYS is required on all programs and other promotional items associated with this play's performance.

When you pay royalties, you are recognizing the hard work that went into creating the play and making a statement that a play is something of value. We think this is important, and we hope that everyone will do the right thing, thus allowing playwrights to generate income and continue to create wonderful new works for the stage.

Plays are owned by the playwrights who wrote them. Violating a playwright's copyright is a very serious matter and violates both United States and international copyright law. Infringement is punishable by actual damages and attorneys' fees, statutory damages of up to $150,000 per incident, and even possible criminal sanctions. **Infringement is theft. Don't do it.**

Have a question about copyright? Please contact us by email at info@youthplays.com or by phone at 424-703-5315. When in doubt, please ask.

CAST OF CHARACTERS

SKYE, girl, age 5-13.
ROCKY, boy, age 5-13.
RATANI, girl, age 5-13.
GRANT, boy, age 5-13.

PRODUCTION NOTES

1. The play consists of a series of scenes featuring the same 4 characters (in different combinations) at ages ranging from 5 through 13 years old.

2. Each scene requires 2, 3, or 4 performers.

3. Your production may choose to perform the play with all scenes in the original order, but it is also permissible to remove scenes or reorder them as suits your needs.

4. The minimum cast size is 4 (2F and 2M), and the maximum cast, if every scene is cast with a different set of actors, is 37 (21F and 16M), with many combinations possible in between.

5. The age ranges noted in each scene are suggestions—directors may use their own discretion when casting, and all roles may be played by age-appropriate actors, or by older actors (high school, college or adult).

6. Individual scenes (there are also 4 monologues) from 1-5 minutes may be selected for use in drama competition.

7. No set is required—the play may be performed on a bare stage.

8. No props or costumes are required.

LIST OF SCENES

Cloud Jumping (1M, 1F)
Bus Stop (1M, 1F)
The Baby Artists, or How to Get a Sister (1M, 1F)
Up, Up and Away (1M, 1F)
Man on the Moon (1M, 1F)
Career Day (2F)
Spit! Slap! Shake! (1M, 1-2F)
Bad Guys (1M, 1F)
Kiss and Tell (2F)
Ditch Me (1M, 1F)
Summer Break (1M, 1F)
Double Dating Trouble (2M, 2F)
Dress, Hair, Flowers? (1M, 1F)
Deluxe Package (2M, 2F)
When the Bell Rings (2M, 2F)

CLOUD JUMPING

(Two 5-8 year olds: SKYE is looking up. ROCKY approaches.)

ROCKY: Whatcha looking at?

SKYE: Babies.

ROCKY: All's I see are clouds.

SKYE: The babies are in the clouds.

ROCKY: Babies can't be in the clouds.

SKYE: Sure they can. The clouds are in heaven.

ROCKY: How do you know?

SKYE: I've been there before.

ROCKY: No you haven't.

SKYE: Have too.

ROCKY: How'd you get there?

SKYE: I was born there.

ROCKY: You can't get born there.

SKYE: Yes you can.

ROCKY: Then how'd you get here?

SKYE: I jumped.

ROCKY: Babies can't jump. They'd get hurt.

SKYE: They jump, but then they fly.

ROCKY: Babies can't fly!

SKYE: When they're born they can!

ROCKY: How come I never seen a baby fly?

SKYE: They only can do it at night.

ROCKY: Babies are scared of the dark.

SKYE: But God makes 'em jump anyway.

ROCKY: God wouldn't do that.

SKYE: He has to, so they can get born.

ROCKY: What if you're too scared to jump?

SKYE: He gives you a push.

(*She does.*)

BUS STOP

(*Two 5-8 year olds: Rocky and Skye enter from opposite directions, backing toward each other center stage, simultaneously waving goodbye to their parents.*)

SKYE: Don't worry, I won't!

ROCKY: Don't worry, I will!

SKYE: Bye Dad!

ROCKY: Bye Mom!

(*They bump into each other.*)

SKYE: Oh! Hi!

ROCKY: Hi.

SKYE: Where is everybody?

ROCKY: We're early.

SKYE: Or late. My Dad's watch is broken.

ROCKY: My Mom's never late 'cause she has to go to work.

SKYE: Except today, maybe she is.

ROCKY: If we were late she'd be mad and she wasn't mad.

SKYE: Then where is everybody?

ROCKY: I bet everybody's sick 'cause of that kid who threw up in the back seat.

SKYE: How come we're not?

ROCKY: 'Cause we didn't get splattered.

SKYE: Oh. *(Beat.)* What happens if we miss the bus?

ROCKY: You get to go home.

SKYE: There's nobody home at my house.

ROCKY: Nobody home at mine either.

SKYE: How you gonna get in?

ROCKY: Climb through a window.

SKYE: What if you can't reach it?

ROCKY: I can.

SKYE: What if you don't fit?

ROCKY: I will.

SKYE: What if you get stuck hanging there all day?

ROCKY: I won't!

SKYE: What if you break the glass and get cut and bleed to death?

ROCKY: That's not gonna happen!

SKYE: It could. *(Beat.)* I've never been home alone. Have you?

ROCKY: Nope. *(Beat.)* I guess if you want you can come with me.

SKYE: I can?

ROCKY: Yeah, I'll give you a boost, and you can climb through the window! C'mon!

THE BABY ARTISTS OR, HOW TO GET A SISTER

(Two 5-8 year olds: Skye has been waiting in line for the swing; Rocky wants to cut.)

ROCKY: Still waiting for the swing?

SKYE: Yup.

ROCKY: Let me cut.

SKYE: What'll you give me?

ROCKY: My ice cream money.

SKYE: There's no ice cream on Tuesday.

ROCKY: Okay, I'll let you use my scented markers in art.

SKYE: Art's not 'til Friday.

ROCKY: Then I'll tell you a secret.

SKYE: What kind?

ROCKY: Where babies come from.

SKYE: I already know.

ROCKY: Bet you don't.

SKYE: My mom told me when I asked for a sister.

ROCKY: Bet she didn't tell you the truth. *(Skye whispers in Rocky's ear:)* That's not how you get a sister!

SKYE: Then where do they come from?

ROCKY: From artists.

SKYE: Artists can't make babies.

ROCKY: Yup. They draw them real careful, then color them in.

SKYE: That's a picture, not a baby.

ROCKY: Put it under the mother's pillow and it turns into a real baby.

SKYE: If that's true why didn't my mom tell me?

ROCKY: Maybe she doesn't want you to get a sister.

SKYE: Maybe not.

ROCKY: Hey, she's done with the swing! Your turn—

SKYE: That's okay, you can cut.

ROCKY: I can?

SKYE: If you let me use your scented markers on Friday!

(Shake or slap hands.)

UP, UP AND AWAY

(Two 5-8 year olds: Skye is looking up as Rocky approaches.)

ROCKY: What's up, Skye?

SKYE: My balloon!

ROCKY: You let it go?

SKYE: My Dad tied it to my wrist real tight, but it escaped!

ROCKY: What color is it?

SKYE: My Dad's favoritist—

ROCKY: Which is...?

SKYE: Blue. Can you see it?

ROCKY: Everything up there's blue.

SKYE: I know. *(Sigh.)* I loved that balloon.

ROCKY: If you cry real hard I bet your Dad'll get you another.

SKYE: I don't want another one! I want that one.

ROCKY: *(Scanning the sky:)* Well, it's gone, all right.

SKYE: Do you think it popped?

ROCKY: Nah, it probably just floated all the way up to heaven by now.

SKYE: You think so? *(Straining to see:)* I wish I could see what heaven looks like —

ROCKY: It's really colorful —

SKYE: How do you know?

ROCKY: Has to be — 'cause all the balloons are up there.

SKYE: I really miss mine.

ROCKY: Well, there's one good thing —

SKYE: There is?

ROCKY: When you die, you'll get it back!

MAN ON THE MOON

(Two 5-8 year olds: Skye is looking up as Rocky approaches.)

SKYE: *(Dreamily:)* Isn't the moon beautiful?

ROCKY: I guess... Bet you don't know what it's made of —

SKYE: Bet you don't.

ROCKY: My Dad told me it's made of cheese.

SKYE: No way.

ROCKY: How do you know?

SKYE: 'Cause all the air would stink of cheese.

ROCKY: American cheese. That doesn't stink at all.

SKYE: My Dad told me it's made of glass.

ROCKY: No way.

SKYE: How do you know?

ROCKY: 'Cause if it got broken all the glass would shoot down on people's heads and cut them.

SKYE: That's why it has to be up so high—so it won't break.

ROCKY: It's not as high as it looks.

SKYE: You can't reach it.

ROCKY: My dad can. He's about this tall. *(Measuring:)* Take about ten of him, one on top of the other, and you'd be there.

SKYE: My Dad's taller than yours, so it'd only take like...six of him.

ROCKY: My Dad has a really high ladder.

SKYE: So does mine. As soon as he gets home, he's gonna climb up and get me the moon, and I'm gonna hold it in my hands, and I won't break it.

ROCKY: My Dad's already home and when he gets there first, I'm gonna have a grilled cheese sandwich! See ya!

CAREER DAY

(Two 5-8 year olds: Skye is sitting, cross-legged with her eyes closed as RATANI approaches.)

RATANI: Wake-up, Skye! You can't sleep on the playground!

SKYE: I'm not sleeping—I'm picturing.

RATANI: What?

SKYE: What I want to be when I grow up.

RATANI: Why?

SKYE: My dad says if I can picture it I can become it.

RATANI: Become what?

SKYE: Lots of things—

RATANI: You can't be lots of things —

SKYE: Who says?

RATANI: God. You have to pick one.

SKYE: I can't pick one.

RATANI: When you're all grown up you have to. So what's it gonna be?

SKYE: I'm going to be a dresser.

RATANI: Huh?

SKYE: Like the lady who changes my Mom's hair color all the time.

RATANI: Good choice!

SKYE: And in my second grow up I'm going to be a dancer —

RATANI: That's not the rules, Skye — you don't get a second grow up.

SKYE: *(Closing her eyes:)* I can picture it *(Opening:)* so I can become it!

RATANI: You can be a dancer or a dresser, but you can't be both!

SKYE: Yes I can, 'cause in my third grow up, guess what?

RATANI: What?

SKYE: I'm going to be God! See ya!

SPIT! SLAP! SHAKE!

(Two 5-8 year olds: Rocky finds Skye on the playground. Depending on your preference, Ratani, same age, may or may not be on stage watching them.)

ROCKY: Hey, Skye! Where you been? We need you in foursquare!

SKYE: I can't! Go away! Quick!

ROCKY: What's wrong with you?

SKYE: Ratani's watching us!

ROCKY: So?

SKYE: She's been spreading rumors!

ROCKY: About what?

SKYE: Us! That we like each other!

ROCKY: We don't?

SKYE: We like each other. But we don't like-like each other. Do we?

ROCKY: Ummmmm...

SKYE: Wait! Don't answer that! She's trying to read our lips!

ROCKY: What should we do?

SKYE: We'll swear on it—make sure she's watching...okay, now repeat after me— *(Exaggerating pronunciation:)* Just... Friends... Forever!

ROCKY: *(As if to Ratani:)* Just... Friends... Forever!

TOGETHER: Spit! Slap! Shake!

(They do.)

ROCKY: And the pact can never be broken!

SKYE: Never?

ROCKY: Ummmmmmm—

SKYE: Quick! While she's not looking—put an expiration date on it—

ROCKY: Like the milk cartons!

SKYE: Yes! Let's see...how about—

ROCKY: Next Tuesday!

(Together — Spit, slap, shake.)

BAD GUYS

(Two 5-8 year olds: Rocky is alone on stage trying out karate moves. Skye enters.)

SKYE: Hey Rocky — whatcha doing?

ROCKY: Practicing.

SKYE: To fight somebody?

ROCKY: Hopefully.

SKYE: Who?

ROCKY: Bad guys.

SKYE: Here?

ROCKY: No! When I grow up.

SKYE: But you told the class you're gonna be an accountant — like your Dad.

ROCKY: That's my back-up plan — my Dad says I should have one.

SKYE: How come?

ROCKY: In case I grow up to be short like him.

SKYE: Listen, do you want to fight bad guys from the bottom of your heart?

ROCKY: Yeah.

SKYE: My Dad says if you can picture it you can become it!

ROCKY: But what if I'm not big enough?

SKYE: Just close your eyes...and picture in your mind growing taller and taller.

(Rocky closes his eyes and seems to grow taller.)

Got it? *(Rocky nods.)* Okay, now picture some bad guys running in!

(Rocky suddenly kicks and punches imagined enemies.)

See? You're doin' it! You're fighting bad guys!

ROCKY: *(Opening his eyes:)* Yeah, but—there's only one problem—

SKYE: What?

ROCKY: I didn't see myself winning.

SKYE: Oh. *(Beat.)* Well, don't worry—you've got a back-up plan!

KISS AND TELL

(Two females, 9-12: Skye is on stage as Ratani, who secretly has a crush on Grant, approaches.)

RATANI: Grant's mad about the rumor going around you know.

SKYE: What rumor?

RATANI: Rocky said you kissed him.

SKYE: When?

RATANI: At the baseball parade.

SKYE: You shouldn't believe everything you hear.

RATANI: Grant says if you did he's breaking up with you.

SKYE: Rocky's just trying to make him jealous!

RATANI: So, you didn't kiss him?

SKYE: Why would I kiss Rocky?

RATANI: He's so cute! I'd kiss Rocky if he asked me.

SKYE: He wouldn't. You're not his type.

RATANI: Yeah, I'm more Grant's type.

SKYE: Too bad he's already taken.

RATANI: Yeah, too bad. Unless you kissed Rocky—

SKYE: If anybody kissed Rocky at the parade it wasn't me.

RATANI: Actually, it was me.

SKYE: What? Where?

RATANI: Behind the dugout.

SKYE: I mean cheek or lips?

RATANI: Lips.

SKYE: You're making that up!

RATANI: Why would I?

SKYE: I can't believe he kissed you too!

RATANI: So you did kiss Rocky at the parade!

SKYE: Not during—after. And I wouldn't have if I knew he kissed you!

RATANI: He actually didn't.

SKYE: Then why'd you say he did?

RATANI: I promised Grant I'd get the truth. See ya!

DITCH ME

(Two 10-12 year olds: GRANT looks dejected as Skye approaches, and he is fidgeting with his thumbs.)

SKYE: Grant, I've been looking everywhere for you!

GRANT: Yeah, right-

SKYE: What's wrong?

GRANT: Ratani said you ditched me —

SKYE: I'd never ditch you!

GRANT: She said you're going home with Rocky instead of me —

SKYE: I came with you, I'm leaving with you.

GRANT: But why'd she say it?

SKYE: Easy — what Ratani wants, Ratani gets.

GRANT: And Ratani wants...what exactly?

SKYE: You — all to herself!

GRANT: No way — I'm not her type.

SKYE: You're totally her type!

GRANT: Rocky's more her type, you know, he's got that hair thing going on...

SKYE: I know!... But you've got...cool t-shirts.

GRANT: Big deal.

SKYE: And that thing you do? With your thumbs? That's really cool —

GRANT: *(Doing it:)* I can't help it, really.

SKYE: Trust me, Ratani's obsessed with you.

GRANT: Then why'd she come to the dance with Rocky?

SKYE: 'Cause you asked me first.

GRANT: Only because I figured she'd say no!

SKYE: Yeah, well, I only said yes 'cause I was afraid Rocky wouldn't ask me.

GRANT: Bummer.

SKYE: Totally. Unless...

GRANT: Yeah?

SKYE: You want me to ditch you?

GRANT: Done!

(High-fiving each other, they exit happily in opposite directions.)

SUMMER BREAK

(Two 9-12 year olds: Skye and Rocky enter together.)

ROCKY: I can't believe I'm not gonna see you for six weeks.

SKYE: Promise you'll write to me?

ROCKY: I promise I'll text you.

SKYE: Letters! My camp doesn't let you bring cells.

ROCKY: So you sneak it in.

SKYE: No way! This girl in my cabin got caught last summer and they made her clean toilets for a week.

ROCKY: That's harsh. I wouldn't go to camp without my phone.

SKYE: If you cared about me you'd write!

ROCKY: If you cared about me you'd bring your cell!

SKYE: The boys at my camp write letters.

ROCKY: That's stupid! Nobody at my camp writes letters. They'll think I'm a loser.

SKYE: Nobody has to know—

ROCKY: They'd know.

SKYE: So, wait 'til they're asleep.

ROCKY: That's what I'm saying—bring your cell and text me when everyone's asleep. That's what the girls at my camp do after lights out.

SKYE: And how do you know that?

ROCKY: Who do you think they're texting?

SKYE: Fine! But I better not get caught!

DOUBLE DATING TROUBLE

(Four 9-12 year olds: Rocky is center stage as Ratani and Grant enter.)

GRANT: Rocky, you have to make up with Skye by tonight!

ROCKY: No way.

RATANI: You have to! My Mom already bought the tickets!

ROCKY: Is she ready to say she's sorry?

GRANT: Yeah—

RATANI: As long as you go first—

ROCKY: Not gonna happen. I went first last time. And the time before that, and the—

RATANI: But I can't go to the movie if Skye isn't going and she won't go unless you say you're sorry!

GRANT: C'mon, Rock—she's really sorry.

ROCKY: How do you know?

RATANI: Trust me, she is! You can read it all over her face! Show him—

(Grant does.)

ROCKY: That's her mad face!

RATANI: He's not doing it right—just meet her and see for yourself.

ROCKY: Tell her if she's ready to say she's sorry first, meet me in the band room before lunch.

(Rocky exits.)

RATANI: This is never going to work!

GRANT: Trust me, it'll work.

(Skye enters.)

Hey, Skye! Rocky wants you to meet him in the band room before lunch.

SKYE: Wild horses couldn't drag me there.

GRANT: What if he's ready to say he's sorry?

SKYE: Is he?

RATANI: If you say you're sorry first—

SKYE: No way. I went first last time! And the time before that and the time before—

RATANI: What's it matter who goes first—

GRANT: As long as you're both sorry?

SKYE: Because I'm only sorry if he's sorry first.

RATANI: Trust me, he is!

SKYE: How do you know?

RATANI: You can read it all over his face! Show her—

(Grant does.)

SKYE: That's his hungry face!

RATANI: Grant's not doing it right—just meet him and see for yourself.

SKYE: Tell Rocky if he's ready to say he's sorry first, he can meet me right here before lunch.

(Grant and Ratani exit. Rocky enters. Awkward silence.)

ROCKY: So, ummm...you have something to tell me?

SKYE: If you have something to tell me first.

ROCKY: Well, I'm really hungry—

SKYE: Well, I'm really mad!

ROCKY: Well, if that's all you have to say, I'm gonna get a slice of pizza before they run out!

SKYE: Well, if that's all you have to say, then go ahead!

(Rocky starts to exit, then, realizing he can't bring himself to leave her standing there, he mumbles something unintelligible.)

(Eagerly:) I'm sorry too! Let's eat!

(They exit together.)

DRESS, HAIR, FLOWERS?

(Two 11-13 year olds: Rocky talks to Ratani.)

ROCKY: Hey Ratani—want to go to the semi-formal with Grant?

RATANI: No way.

ROCKY: It's a paying gig.

RATANI: Yeah? How much?

ROCKY: Both tickets—

RATANI: Dress? Hair? Flowers?

ROCKY: Everything!

RATANI: Flow-ers, right? Not one lousy rose?

ROCKY: A whaddyacallit—a whole bouquet.

RATANI: White calla lilies?

ROCKY: Whatever!

RATANI: Sorry. I can't. Skye broke up with Max and I said I'd stay home with her.

ROCKY: She won't care.

RATANI: She's my best friend.

ROCKY: I'll get her a date.

RATANI: She's broke too.

ROCKY: A paying gig—

RATANI: Both tickets?

ROCKY: Yeah.

RATANI: Dress? Hair? Flowers?

ROCKY: A dozen long-stemmed red roses.

RATANI: Wow. Cool. I'll ask her.

ROCKY: Ah, I already did.

RATANI: Who's the guy?

ROCKY: Me.

RATANI: You? What'd she say?

ROCKY: Yes, but only if Grant takes you. So? Do we have a deal?

RATANI: What about the limo?

ROCKY: What limo?

RATANI: No limo, no deal.

ROCKY: What color?

RATANI: I don't know. Surprise us!

DELUXE PACKAGE

(Four 12-13 year olds: it's picture day—each character speaks as if to the photographer.)

RATANI: *(Confidently:)* Hi! Aren't you the same photographer as last year? Wow! I didn't think you'd be back after the incident with Todd Bright. Can you believe he wasn't even suspended? *(Posing:)* I love picture day! Not everybody does, but I do, because I come prepared. I remind all my friends, but nobody listens. It's like they just roll out of bed and say, oh, it's picture day, guess I better brush my teeth. Like it's too much hassle to pick an outfit the day before? Make sure it's clean? Comb your hair? *(Posing:)* My friend Rocky, he woke up with a big pimple right here—so he pretended he was sick, but the nurse sent him back to class just in time for pictures. I told him, don't worry—that's why they invented retouching! *(Posing:)* You have my form, right? I checked Package A+ Deluxe with the Misty Blue background—the gray would look really pukey with my dress, don't you think? *(Smoothing her dress with her hands:)* My father let me buy it even though my mother says I'll never wear it again. And these shoes—they weren't even on sale! He might not have told her about the shoes yet. *(Posing:)* What do you mean it's just a headshot? You're kidding! Wow, he's gonna be bummed. *(Posing:)* Are you sure you got a good one? Great! Well, I hope for your sake Todd Bright's out sick today. Bye!

(Ratani exits.)

ROCKY: *(Reluctantly:)* Hi. *(Adjusting his collar:)* Ummm, sorry, I forgot to fill out my form—maybe we should just skip the picture... Oh, okay. *(A sigh, then a half-hearted pose and a flurry of blinking:)* Sorry—that always happens to me. *(Half-hearted pose without blinking:)* Huh? I thought I was smiling. Okay... *(Adding a fake smile:)* Is that it? Ummmm, I think my mother prefers glossy. Size? She usually wants like the smallest package you have—one wallet should do it. Oh, and, do you have retouching? Yeah, she wants to add some of that. Okay, so, we're good to go?

(Rocky exits.)

GRANT: *(Casually:)* Hola! I love picture day — we get to miss Spanish! Sweet! You look familiar — wait — I recognize you! You do all our school portraits! So, do you do this by choice? *(Posing:)* I mean, was this your main career path, or a back-up? Can you make a living at it, or do you have a real job? Nah, I didn't bother to fill out the form — my mom uses a professional for all our family photos. I mean, like, we go to a whatever-you-call-it — a studio. You have a studio? Cool. I'll tell her. *(Posing:)* We're done? That was fast. You can take some more if you want — Spanish isn't even over yet. Well, have a good year then — oh! Okay then, have a good life! Gracias!

(Grant exits.)

SKYE: *(Wistfully:)* Wow, I can't even believe it — my last picture day in middle school! My mother says you take the best pictures of all the school photographers. The one you took of me in first grade's my favorite — I had on my blue flowered dress with the little heart buttons. Her favorite's the one you took of me last year. I just wish I didn't wear yellow! My mother thinks it's my color, but she's totally wrong. I wanted to come to picture re-take day but she wouldn't let me. As you can see, I'm not wearing yellow. But I'm not having the best hair day. Up or down — I couldn't decide. I should have had it cut. In homeroom my friend Ratani said I should wear it up, and in health Grant said definitely down, and in math Rocky said part up, part down, and, well, you can see how it all turned out. Okay, I guess I'm ready. *(Posing:)* Wait! I'm not! This is hard — I mean, coming up with the right expression for my last picture in middle school ever. *(Posing:)* How was that? Okay, well, I'll see you next year! What? You don't do the high school pictures? *(Beat.)* I guess this is goodbye then... *(She starts to exit, then:)* Unless my hair looks horrible — then I'll see you make up day — no matter what! Okay, well...bye!

(Skye exits.)

WHEN THE BELL RINGS

(Four 12-13 year olds: Skye stares straight ahead and taps her foot to the beat of a clock.)

ROCKY: *(Entering:)* C'mon, Skye—let's get out of here!

SKYE: The bell hasn't rung yet—

ROCKY: We never wait for the bell.

SKYE: We have to—it's the last time it'll ever ring for us in middle school.

ROCKY: We're not talking the end of the world, Skye—

SKYE: As we know it, yes!

ROCKY: Finally! We're high schoolers now!

SKYE: Not until the bell rings.

ROCKY: No way—class is over, middle school's over, I'm outta here—

SKYE: Fine. Go without me.

ROCKY: I don't want to go without you.

SKYE: Have the last three years here meant nothing to you?

ROCKY: Ummmmmm...I mean, yeah, of course they've meant something...

SKYE: Then, out of respect, we can at least wait for the last bell.

(Ratani enters.)

RATANI: You guys—what're you waiting for?

SKYE: Closure.

RATANI: Huh?

ROCKY: Have the last three years here meant nothing to you?

RATANI: My sister said she give us a ride if we hurry up.

SKYE: Soon as the bell rings —

(Grant enters.)

GRANT: Your sister says she's leaving if we don't hurry up —

RATANI: Apparently, we need closure.

GRANT: Huh?

ROCKY: Don't worry — it's gonna ring any second now —

SKYE: We need a picture!

GRANT: Guys, please —

ROCKY: *(As if to someone in audience:)* Hey, excuse me —

RATANI: Can you take our picture?

SKYE: Okay, smile everybody!

(They smile and pose, arms around each other. Grant, Ratani and Rocky put rabbit ears behind Skye's head.)

ROCKY: Say, goodbye middle school!

ALL: Goodbye middle school!

(Flash — they freeze for a beat — BELL RINGS.)

RATANI: I guess that's it.

GRANT: Yup, that's it.

ROCKY: It's official.

SKYE: *(Sigh.)* I'm gonna miss this place.

ROCKY: Yeah. Me too.

RATANI: Jeez... It went by so fast. Do you think high school's gonna go too fast?

(Beat.)

ALL: Nah!

(All exit together, arm in arm. End of play.)

The Author Speaks

What inspired you to write this play?
I'm a lifelong passionate diarist, and the diaries I've kept for my three children for twenty-three years were the inspiration for many of the scenes, characters, and dialogue. After writing my book, *Before You Forget, The Wisdom of Writing Diaries for Your Children*, published in 2001, I loved the raw material of the diaries too much to leave it alone. However, without the prompt from Janet Milstein, an editor for Smith & Kraus, I might never have written **The Adventures of Rocky & Skye**. Janet was seeking one-minute comic duets to be included in an anthology, and I decided to take a shot at writing some. She enthusiastically accepted *Cloud Jumping*, and *The Baby Artists* which I wrote from diary entries I had written to my son when he was seven (now published in the *Winners Competition Series V.2: Award-Winning 90-Second Comic Scenes Ages 4-12*, 2010, edited by Janet Milstein, Smith & Kraus publishers). Rocky & Skye delighted me, and I liked the challenging hit and run format of the short comic scene. Scenes from different developmental ages kept coming to me, and I realized Rocky, Skye, Ratani and Grant were growing up, just as my own three children had—but the constant was their friendship and their emotional bond.

Was the structure of the play influenced by any other work?
The structure was influenced by the idea of short comic scenes using language that young performers could easily master in performance and competition, but that would reflect the thoughts and feelings of real kids in ordinary conflicts inspired by going to school and making friends.

Have you dealt with the same theme in other works that you have written?
Definitely. In the original diaries, yes, that's what I've paid attention to in writing to my kids—as if speaking directly, one-on-one, to each of them at the age they're at when I'm writing to them, capturing their exact words, beliefs, questions, feelings, philosophy, conflicts, answers, innocence, *and* wisdom. In *The Adventures of Rocky & Skye* I created real life characters who experience ordinary joy and ordinary pain, who seize the possibility for playfulness and curiosity each moment, plan their future, value relationships, and celebrate the beauty and mystery of life through the child's point of view.

What do you hope to achieve with this work?
I hope *The Adventures of Rocky & Skye* inspires young actors to take a risk on stage. I hope the stories of friends going to school and growing up amuses and charms parents, as well as kids, and that adults will be reminded of special moments from their childhood and inspired to share those with their children. I hope this play reminds audiences to appreciate the poetic moments of childhood and friendship.

What are the most common mistakes that occur in productions of your work?
This play was designed to be easily produced without props, costume, or set. However, an astute director will find many opportunities for theatricality with *The Adventures of Rocky & Skye*. "Simple" doesn't have to mean *easy* or obvious or static or non-theatrical—there's potential for physical comedy and emotional depth. Interesting choices can be made in terms of casting, which is quite flexible.

What inspired you to become a playwright?
I always wanted to be a writer, but instead of getting an MFA right after college, I decided to get an M.Ed. and become a counselor, and I maintained a private counseling practiced for many years. During this time I entered training as a psychodramatist (and became certified) — using spontaneous dramatic enactments as a form of therapy in groups. The storytelling and theatricality of these healing experiences inspired my return to writing. I love the immediacy and directness of writing dialogue — writing in the present tense, the here and now.

How did you research the subject?
I didn't need to do research this play which is drawn from life, but I tried the scenes out — many times — with kids, revising and fine-tuning to make sure kids could and would speak (memorize and deliver) the lines and that the conflicts and scenes and language aroused laughter, smiles, appreciation.

Are any characters modeled after real life or historical figures?
Rocky and Skye are modeled after my son and daughters, Landon (now 23), Perri (19), and Franci (14).

Shakespeare gave advice to the players in *Hamlet*; if you could give advice to your cast what would it be?
Come from your heart. Find your feeling connection to the character/scene and play it. Go for subtlety in the humor — be real and it'll be funny. Pay attention to levels — find them, express them.

About the Author

Kelly DuMar is an award-winning playwright, creative arts workshop facilitator and author of a non-fiction book for parents, *Before You Forget — The Wisdom of Writing Diaries for*

Your Children. Kelly's plays have been produced around the US and in Canada, and her award winning one-act plays and monologues have been published by a variety of publishers. Kelly is a long-time member and past president of Playwrights' Platform, Boston, and she produces the annual Our Voices Festival of Boston area women playwrights. Kelly received her Master's Degree in Education from the Harvard University Graduate School of Education and her BA in English with Honors from the University of Massachusetts at Amherst. Kelly is a certified psychodramatist and Fellow in the American Society for Group Psychotherapy, and she is artistic director of The Red Suitcase Playerz, a Playback Theatre Troupe for kids. She lives in the Boston area with her husband and three children.

About YouthPLAYS

YouthPLAYS (www.youthplays.com) is a publisher of award-winning professional dramatists and talented new discoveries, each with an original theatrical voice, and all dedicated to expanding the vocabulary of theatre for young actors and audiences. On our website you'll find one-act and full-length plays and musicals for teen and pre-teen (and even college) actors, as well as duets and monologues for competition. Many of our authors' works have been widely produced at high schools and middle schools, youth theatres and other TYA companies, both amateur and professional, as well as at elementary schools, camps, churches and other institutions serving young audiences and/or actors worldwide. Most are intended for performance by young people, while some are intended for adult actors performing for young audiences.

YouthPLAYS was co-founded by professional playwrights Jonathan Dorf and Ed Shockley. It began merely as an additional outlet to market their own works, which included a substantial body of award-winning published and unpublished plays and musicals. Those interested in their published plays were directed to the respective publishers' websites, and unpublished plays were made available in electronic form. But when they saw the desperate need for material for young actors and audiences—coupled with their experience that numerous quality plays for young people weren't finding a home—they made the decision to represent the work of other playwrights as well. Dozens and dozens of authors are now members of the YouthPLAYS family, with scripts available both electronically and in traditional acting editions. We continue to grow as we look for exciting and challenging plays and musicals for young actors and audiences.

About ProduceaPlay.com

Let's put up a play! Great idea! But producing a play takes time, energy and knowledge. While finding the necessary time and energy is up to you, ProduceaPlay.com is a website designed to assist you with that third element: knowledge.

Created by YouthPLAYS' co-founders, Jonathan Dorf and Ed Shockley, ProduceaPlay.com serves as a resource for producers at all levels as it addresses the many facets of production. As Dorf and Shockley speak from their years of experience (as playwrights, producers, directors and more), they are joined by a group of award-winning theatre professionals and experienced teachers from the world of academic theatre, all making their expertise available for free in the hope of helping this and future generations of producers, whether it's at the school or university level, or in community or professional theatres.

The site is organized into a series of major topics, each of which has its own page that delves into the subject in detail, offering suggestions and links for further information. For example, Publicity covers everything from Publicizing Auditions to How to Use Social Media to Posters to whether it's worth hiring a publicist. Casting details Where to Find the Actors, How to Evaluate a Resume, Callbacks and even Dealing with Problem Actors. You'll find guidance on your Production Timeline, The Theater Space, Picking a Play, Budget, Contracts, Rehearsing the Play, The Program, House Management, Backstage, and many other important subjects.

The site is constantly under construction, so visit often for the latest insights on play producing, and let it help make your play production dreams a reality.

More from YouthPLAYS

Dear Chuck by Jonathan Dorf
Dramedy. 30-40 minutes. 8-30+ performers (gender flexible).

Teenagers are caught in the middle—they're not quite adults, but they're definitely no longer children. Through scenes and monologues, we meet an eclectic group of teens trying to communicate with that wannabe special someone, coping with a classmate's suicide, battling controlling parents, swimming for that island of calm in the stormy sea of technology—and many others. What they all have in common is the search for their "Chuck," that elusive moment of knowing who you are. Also available in a 60-70 minute version.

Warriors by Hayley Lawson-Smith
Drama. 40-50 minutes. 4 females, 1 male.

Not every hero gets a song or the cheers of the crowd—or even acknowledgement. In Zordana's land, a hero fights bravely in the open field, destroying monsters and dark magic. In Amy's world, her hero is the sister who takes care of her. Maddie's hero is her brother, who may tease her mercilessly but loves her dearly. As tragedy threatens to consume their separate worlds, only in coming together can they battle back the dark.

The Superhero Ultraferno by Don Zolidis
Comedy. 30-40 minutes. 6-20 females, 6-20 males (12-50+ performers).

Now that nerds have taken over the world, it's imperative that all popular kids learn everything they can about comic book superheroes. Join two nerds and a crack team of actors as they race hilariously through the world of tights-wearing crimefighters, from the 1960s TV Batman to the soap opera insanity of the Fantastic Four to a bizarre, German opera of Spiderman. Also available as a full-length.

Murder (Comedy) in Space! by Ed Shockley
Comedy. About 50 minutes. Flexible ensemble of 9-30.

In a zany homage to Inspector Clouseau, with a plot created by middle school students, a bumbling detective and his laser happy cohorts teleport across the galaxy to investigate the death of a futuristic champion of non-violence. The trail leads to the badlands of Mars, where the characters—and the audience—must decide if they will reveal the truth and destroy a fragile intergalactic peace or collaborate in a well-intentioned deception...

Herby Alice Counts Down to Yesterday by Nicole B. Adkins
Comedy. 30-35 minutes. 3 females, 3 males, 4-20+ either (10-50+ performers possible).

Middle school rocket scientist Herby Alice has ambitions as big as the universe, and no time for interviews. Rose Plum, media hopeful, needs a juicy story to get in good with the school broadcast elite. How far is she willing to go to be a star? Or will mad scientists, aliens, befuddled teachers, demanding executives, and the space-time continuum overrun the show?

The Unscary Ghost by Matt Buchanan
Comedy. 40-50 minutes. 5+ females, 3+ males (13-30+ performers possible).

Loosely based on Oscar Wilde's *The Canterville Ghost*. When the Otis family moves into the old Victorian home in Canterville, Ohio, they soon learn that the place is haunted—by a ghost who can't scare anyone. The jaded, modern family alternately taunts and tries to exploit the unfortunate ghost, Simon Canter, even trying to get a spot on the hit TV show, *America's Most Haunted*. Only the oldest daughter, Ginny, seems to care for or understand poor Simon. Can she help him find peace? A sometimes zany, sometimes touching show for the whole family.

Made in the USA
Columbia, SC
19 June 2024